A Christian Understanding of Daily Work

Graham Dow

Bishop of Willesden

GROVE BOOKS LIMITED

RIDLEY HALL RD CAMBRIDGE CB3 9HU

Contents

The Purpose of this Booklet

This booklet is intended to help Christian people consider the place of their daily occupation in the purposes of God. Perhaps it will help to redress the great neglect of this subject in our churches.

It is intended that the booklet can be used for a group study course. A guide to its use in this way is provided on page 14. The centre four pages can be removed and photocopied (and enlarged) for distribution beforehand so that participants can come to the group meetings prepared. Alternatively, the answers to the questions can be written in the booklet itself.

The word 'occupation' is preferred because 'work' is easily understood as paid employment. The discussion must include homemakers, those in voluntary work, the retired and those who need employment but are unable to find it.

The aim of this booklet is not to consider Sunday trading, corruption, or unemployment—to name some of the well known points at issue concerning employment patterns. It is to discuss the shape of God's purposes for all human beings, (not only Christians), and how, in fitting those purposes, daily occupations should be given right direction.

The Cover Illustration is by Peter Ashton

First Impression March 1994
Second Impression February 1997
ISSN 0144-171X
ISBN 1 85174 261 1

1
The Importance of the Subject

In the minds of most Christians in our churches there is a deep cleavage between the purposes of God and the world of secular reality. The purposes of God are seen as about people becoming Christians, living holy lives and serving other people. There is little thought of God having purposes in the warp and woof of society as a whole, purposes which embrace all human beings and not only Christians.

When I was on the staff of a college training people for the ordained ministry, I asked students to write about their former occupation. They were to tackle such questions as:

1. What is the purpose of God for human beings as seen in that occupation?
2. What sin lies at the heart of the relationships and structures which make up the social aspect of that employment?
3. Is the purpose of the organization consistent with the direction of the kingdom of God?

I received essays about a wide range of jobs from teaching to journalism, from accountancy to hairdressing. In almost every case the students wrote about being a Christian witness in their work situation, but had nothing at all to say about the purpose of God for people in their occupation as an occupation. They saw the call of God as about getting to work on time, not pinching the office stationery and witnessing about Christ to those they worked alongside. They did not see that the whole work enterprise belongs to what God has commanded human beings to do in his world. It is part of his design for the world as he intends it to be.

These potential clergy were unable to see any connection between the purposes of God and what they had actually been doing. They could not see that computer technology or hairdressing or brewing or rolling steel had anything to do with God and his purposes. Presumably, in their churches, they had never had any teaching which helped them to make the connections.

Reasons for Poor Connections Between Faith and Occupations

There are several reasons which have contributed to the serious neglect of these connections.

Firstly, in our Sunday worship there is hardly any reference to the occupations that will take up most of the time in the lives of the congregation in the week that follows. It is not surprising, therefore, if many people feel very unsupported by the church in these occupations.

There are some who do not wish to be faced in church with the issues about their daily occupations; they come to get away from all this, they say. Though this is understandable, it is not to be encouraged. Christians need to pray together in church about their situations in daily life, supporting each other in the difficulties and hearing the word of God as it addresses those situations.

Secondly, for many years daily work was taken for granted. It was considered to be a duty and was, generally speaking, available. Christian concern was taken up with the life of the church. As social concern became more evident in the churches it was the specific problem of unemployment which received attention rather than a broader consideration of the meaning of work.

Thirdly, the most serious reason is the deficiency in our teaching. There is insufficient grasp of what God is making people to be, people in society, people in the world as a whole, and the part work has in that divine purpose.

Reasons for Giving Attention to the Issue

1. The Place of Work in the Purposes of God

If faith and daily life are to be properly integrated, Christian people must have a good understanding of how their occupation fits with God's purposes. They will then be ready to see themselves as servants of God in that occupation just as much as in 'church' work.

Christian people who see that their occupation is important to God in his purposes for a healthy world are helped to have a positive outlook on their daily work routine.

And with a good understanding of the direction of God's purposes through work Christian people can make a more constructive contribution to the work patterns in their place of work.

2. Daily Working Life and Sunday Worship

We need to give greater prominence to the realities of daily working life in the context of our Sunday services. We are seriously open to the charge that our worship is irrelevant when it relates so little to the daily working week of most of the church members.

3. The Gospel as a Challenge to the Prevailing Values of Society

The gospel presents a challenge to the prevailing values on which our society and its institutions are based. Moreover, this challenge needs to be presented publicly.

With over 2 million people unemployed we have a serious social problem. To be without paid employment not only reduces income for most people to little more than subsistence level, but it also sets them in a position of sharp contrast in status and income from those who are in employment. Those without employment suffer serious loss of self-esteem and meaning in their lives, a loss placed upon them by force of circumstances.

Secondly, serious stress is developing in our nation. Many of those who are in work are being worked harder and harder for longer and longer hours. A recent survey showed that in Britain the percentage of men working over 46 hours a week is 42%, the highest in Western Europe, whereas in Germany it is 14%.[1] This is having an effect in our churches: attendance at midweek church meetings has declined because of these pressures.

Thirdly, most of our institutions are in crisis as one change follows another with great rapidity. Here again is great potential for stress of which the government seems unaware.

There is a broader phenomenon behind these kinds of issues. As Lesslie Newbigin and others have argued, the energy of 300 years of rationalism is running out.[2] Religious truth has come to be treated as a purely personal decision. Only what can be established as empirical, scientific truth can be accepted as common truth. The logic of this critical process is that this fundamental premise itself has to be questioned and we are left with nothing we can hold on to. The process, ultimately, destroys itself. We are left with utter confusion as to the purpose and meaning of life.

What is needed, according to Newbigin, as in the time of Augustine, is a reinterpretation of the world starting from the basic Christian truth of the resurrection, a proclamation of the truth found in the scriptures. The gospel is truth, public truth, not purely personal values. Its truth must be proclaimed in all areas of life in the confidence that, in the present vacuum of agreed truth, its convictions will carry.

This booklet seeks to offer gospel and scriptural truth to assist in the understanding of the meaning of our daily occupations.

1 As reported in *The Times*, 10th June 1991, indicating the findings of an Equal Opportunities Commission survey, citing as source Eurostat 1990.
2 L Newbigin, *The Gospel as Public Truth* (London: SPCK, 1991).

2

What God is Making Human Beings to Be

God has always had a purpose for people as a whole, a pattern for human society, and not simply for what belongs to the life of the church. The Bible is full of indications as to what that purpose is. We find it in the order of creation, the vision of the kingdom of God and in the patterns of God's redemptive work.

Creation Order

Concerning the place of work in the purposes of God for human beings, the creation accounts are a particularly fruitful source of insights. Christian tradition does not accept that the creation pattern is completely destroyed by the fall. Creation remains the ground for argument as Jesus indicates in the discussion about divorce (Mark 10.6-9). On the other hand there is no mention of any time scale in Genesis between creation and fall, so it would seem that we are not intended to romanticize about an age of primordial bliss. The presentation of the ruin immediately following the creation suggests rather that we are to interpret the world in the light of creation-and-fall—that is, we are to view human society through the interpretative keys of both creation and fall, held firmly together.

In relation to work, the pattern of creation indicates that it is our privilege, dignity and responsibility as human beings to develop the world under God (Gen 1.28). The pattern of the fall, however, indicates that work becomes simply a sweat to stay alive (Gen 3.19). So the two essential principles offer us opposite extremes and the whole range of human work lies somewhere in the range between them, interpreted in the light of both.

The Vision of the Kingdom of God

Throughout Scripture the goal of God's purposes is the coming kingdom of God. As a promise of perfect harmony the kingdom is expressed as righteousness and peace in daily life. Jesus announced that the kingdom has arrived with his presence and is to be proclaimed by his followers. Yet he also teaches that we are to pray for the kingdom to come. It is both here now and not yet. We are to seek its marks in every walk of life.

The History of God's Redemptive Work

Since the pattern of creation has been greatly distorted by the fall of humankind through sin, the purpose of God for human society is seen in the consistent direction of all God's redemptive work, from the laws given to Old Testament Israel, to the life in the Spirit bursting forth in the New Testament church.

Here in the pattern of what God is making us to be lies the basis of all human rights and duties; for all people have a right to enter into that which God has purposed for them and a right to be allowed to do so by their fellow human beings.

3
The Purpose of Work I: Creative Management of God's World

In Genesis chapter 1 we read:

> 'Let us make humankind in our image…let them rule over all the creatures…male and female he created them…'
> 'Be fruitful and increase in number; fill the earth and subdue it. Rule over…every living creature.'
> 'I give you every plant…for food.'
> 'God saw all that all that he had made, and it was very good.'
> 'By the seventh day God had finished the work he had been doing; so on the seventh day he rested from all his work.' (1.26-2.2)

In the Genesis 2 account the man is placed in a well-watered garden where trees are pleasant to the sight and good for food. The man is told to work the garden and take care of it (2.15).

Important connections are indicated here between work and creativity, work and leisure, work and satisfaction, work and human community, work and livelihood, work and the product, work and worship.

Work and Creativity

(i) Partnership with God in our Daily Occupation: My Work as God's Work

The Genesis accounts see God's intended pattern for people everywhere as partnership with him. It is as if he says: 'I have made the world and I have made you; now rule over the world for me and with me.' The answer given in Genesis 1 to the question, 'Why did God create me?' is 'To manage his world.' Our daily occupation, or daily work, is an expression of this partnership.

Genesis 1 presents God as completing his creation in six days and then resting for one day. It is not necessary to believe that the creation took place in six solar days. The presentation is schematic. The six working days are the same as in the instructions given to God's people in the fourth of the Ten Commandments, to do all their work in six days and to rest on the seventh day, (Exodus 20.8-11). So God is presented in Genesis 1 as 'God the Worker;' and human beings are like this because they are in the image of God. God is the archetypal worker, the one in whom all human work finds its meaning. Human work, therefore cannot be understood apart from God's work in creation. Our work is meant to be a reflection of his creativity. The work we are to do in our daily occupation is God's work; we are partners with him in it.

(ii) Partnership with God in Developing Ourselves and the World: Creative Management

Since we are in the image of God whose work is both creative and satisfying we may conclude that our human work to develop the world is also intended to be creative and satisfying. 'Fill the earth and subdue it.' In other words, 'Use its minerals, its animals, its water, its energy; use the earth and make things.' Creative management is a good description of this divine purpose for us. It is creative because we are in God's image; it is management because we are told to rule the world and develop it. This is the ideal for each person's daily occupation.

The whole growth of civilization is an exciting story of human beings realizing through work the potential with which God made them. As Pope John Paul II says:

> 'The expression "subdue the earth" has an immense range. It means all the resources that the earth (and indirectly the visible world) contains and which, through the conscious activity of man, can be discovered and used for his ends. And so these words, placed at the beginning of the Bible, never cease to be relevant. They embrace equally the past ages of civilization and economy, as also the whole of modern reality and future phases of development, which are perhaps already to some extent beginning to take shape, though for the most part they are still almost unknown to man and hidden from him.'[3]

Work is fundamental to being human and to the development of humanity in accordance with its potential. The point is well made by Tony Dyson as he holds in view the particular effect upon people of industrial and technological development:

> 'By work man has not only begun to transform the face of the earth, but has also himself developed in striking ways as a human being, through the major choices about, and major changes in, his environment which he is now enabled to make. In a word, through work, intervention in the quality of human life is possible on a scale never before imaginable.'[4]

Work is our privilege and responsibility; it belongs to our dignity as humans. As Dyson says, it is our humanization. A whole cluster of phrases can be used to describe work from a theological point of view. It is wealth creation. It is also our stewardship of God's world, and our collaboration or partnership with him.

We may summarize:

Human work is sharing in God's work: it is the expenditure of human energy in the mastery of the world and the development of human life, using the resources of God's creation.

3 John Paul II, *Laborem Exercens* (London: Catholic Truth Society, 1981) p 15.
4 A O Dyson, 'Theology of Work,' in Michael Atkinson (ed), *Mission in Industrial Society* (London: Church House Publishing, 1978) p 41.

Work and Satisfaction

In the creation account God expresses his satisfaction with what he has created and recognizes that it is good. There is here both a satisfaction of the worker and a satisfaction for all humanity. As well as the development of wealth the aim of the work process must be satisfaction and human well-being. Questions like, 'Does my occupation use my potential as a human being?' are important. 'Does it encourage my personal development?' or 'Does it restrict me?' 'Does it even crush my initiative or my creativity?'

There is also the question of whether or not the work enterprise in which I share is for the good of humanity as a whole. The Pope says clearly that work is for people, not people for work.[5] It is for our good and to develop us. We are not here to do it just because it has got to be done.

Work and the Product

Like God we are intended to take delight in our own creativity. This means that we should be able to see what we have achieved and be pleased with it. Sadly, for reasons of supposed economic efficiency, some work patterns have denied this satisfaction to those who work. Paid employment has then become simply the means to an income so that leisure may be enjoyed. It should not surprise us if those who spend many hours of the day in this sort of unfulfilling work show a dulled sense of creative initiative in their lives as a whole. We are simply reaping what we have sown. Car manufacturers like Volvo and Fiat have wisely changed their assembly line patterns to harness the interest of their work force.

Work and Leisure

The creation accounts help us not to divorce our understanding of work from rest or leisure. In the second creation account it is striking that the beauty of the surroundings is described before the instruction is given to work the garden. Leisure, in the sense of sheer enjoyment of what God has made, would seem then to be of the highest esteem in human life. We need have no hesitation about increasing the hours available for leisure as technology displaces human labour.

The division between work, leisure and rest is not, in practice, a simple one. When work is creative and gives pleasure, then rest is the correlative offered in the first creation account. When work is largely sweat and boredom, then leisure becomes the focus of creative opportunities in life. Work, then, becomes difficult to define and cannot be restricted to paid employment. Creative working leisure is to be preferred to dehumanizing paid employment. The present unemployment situation presents us with the challenge of drawing out creative working leisure as well as of creating new jobs. The opportunity is there to give work a new definition along the lines indicated above.

5 John Paul II, *op cit*, pp 22, 23.

Work and Livelihood

It is also significant that the creation account offers a close connection between work and human livelihood. The instinct for self-preservation is thought to be the strongest of human instincts. Consequently, where there is a firm connection between work and livelihood it will help to draw out the scope of human responsibility for work. Presumably this was God's intention. However, the fallen pattern of society means that if a person can obtain livelihood without work, he may do so, thereby falling short of his obligation to God and to other people (see 1 Thess 3.10). The availability of livelihood without the requirement of work is bound to reduce the motivation to work. On the other hand, if the connection between work and livelihood is to be restored, opportunity for paid employment must be available.

The pattern of creation order points to two fundamental mistakes that we have made in our society. First, we have paid some people too little to live on, an inadequate share of what God has given to all. Secondly, we have given it to them without requiring work in return. In view of the highly necessary developments to our roads and railways, if we are to compete efficiently in Europe, this failure to harness our potential labour supply seems very foolish. When we add to this that those who earn pay tax and buy goods, such a policy could do much to stimulate the economy.

Questions

1. Does my occupation encourage my personal development or is it dehumanizing? If the second, what can I do about it?

2. If our society is to find a correct interrelationship between work, income and leisure, what changes would we press for?

My Work as God's Work?

Study Questions for Thinking Through My Daily Occupation

1. Basic description of my job(s) or role(s)
eg teacher, accountant, machine operator, student, housewife, retired, unemployed, voluntary work.

2. What sort of person does this require me to be?
eg thinking, feeling, creative; a servant of others; managerial; morally decisive; able to work with others; almost a robot; morally compromising.

3. What essential aspects of my human potential are not drawn out by my job?
eg responsibility; contribution to society; interests in life; sense of belonging to others; enjoyment of nature.

4. What pressures are there in my job which drive me and others to do what is not right?
eg people are selfish, greedy, dishonest; work is hard and tiring; Christians are persecuted; I get insufficient support; the system forces us to be ruthless (eg business competition); I am told what to do.

5. (a) Who has 'power' to control what happens in my situation?

(b) Who is frustrated by feeling powerless to bring about changes?

6. What 'values' are chosen to justify that use of power?
eg we have to make the highest profit; we do not have time to discuss things; we are 'in charge'; avoiding conflict or anxiety.

How acceptable is that justification from a Christian point of view?

7. What is the aim of my occupation? Does it serve the well-being of people in general?

8. If God were to perfect my daily occupation today, what would I look for him to do?

A Study Course Using this Booklet

(Photocopying pages (i)-(iii))

1. Participants should fill in their answers to the questions on pages (i)–(iii) before the group meets. These pages may be photocopied. It is also better if the appropriate chapters of this booklet are read before the meeting—though they can be read at the meeting.
2. Each week could include a time of discussion about the issues raised by working in one of the fields represented in the group—say, education , law, industry, transport, health care, services, homemaking, and unemployment and retirement. Ask the questions, 'What needs to be challenged in the practice of this occupation?' 'Where does power lie?'
3. Although the questions are more difficult for homemakers, the retired and those who are unemployed they are not impossible if tackled imaginatively.

Week 1
Preliminary reading: chapters 1, 2, 3.
Share answers to questions 1-3, page (i. (If the group is large it is wise for answers to be shared first in pairs so that everyone gets involved. Then there can be a fuller sharing in the group as a whole.)
Bible study: Genesis 1.26-2.3; 2.8-14.
Answer the questions on page 10.
Discussion of issues concerning one occupation.

Week 2
Preliminary reading: chapter 4.
Share answers to questions 4-6, pages (ii), (iii).
Bible study: Gen 2.15-17; 3.1-3,16-18; Amos 5.6-15; 8.4-7; Lk 12.15-21
Answer the questions on page 18.
Discussion of issues concerning one occupation.

Week 3
Preliminary reading: chapter 5.
Share answers to questions 7 and 8, page (iii).
Bible study: Isaiah 9.6, 7.
Discussion of issues concerning one occupation.

Week 4
Preliminary reading: chapter 6.
Bible study: Ephesians 4.17-32.
Answer the question on page 24.
Discussion of issues concerning one occupation.

Week 5
Return to the questions on pages (i)-(iii) and come with answers to them in terms of what you do in your church (if different from your normal occupation). Share your answers.
Discussion of issues concerning one occupation.
Items not covered in previous weeks because of time.

4

The Purpose of Work II: Moral Management for the Good of All

Work and Human Community

It is not always noticed that the creation instructions were given not simply to individuals but to humankind as a whole. 'Let them...' 'Creative management' of the world is something that we do together. The first creation account reflects a sense of the corporateness of humanity as God has created it; the phrase 'in the image of God' is used of the whole of created humanity together, and not just of each individual. The same point is made in the New Testament where corporate language is used to say that the company of Christian believers grows up into the stature of 'the one complete man,' Christ, (Eph 4.13,15). There is therefore no excuse for thinking of our responsibility to work primarily in individual terms. Together we are in the image of God; together we can achieve things that would be impossible single-handed. Responsibility for the task should be shared as much as possible by all, and what we achieve should be for the well-being of all.

Emil Brunner emphasized that as well as the fundamental equality of all in creation, (made in the image of God), there is also a fundamental inequality or, better, 'distinctiveness.'[6] Created with different gifts we make our skills available to each other for the common good. A great many occupations can be understood as service of one another. There are many references in Scripture to the role of the servants of God, references which repay study with one's occupation in mind. Service expresses love, the love which binds people together in unity, meeting each other's needs and tackling a common task.

In order for people in community to achieve goals together, social structures are necessary. It is consistent with the creation order that these should be participative for all so that all can fulfil the responsibility given to them by God to develop his world. But the structures also must enable goals to be reached.

Whereas the structures of government in Western countries are generally participatory (democratic), this is not so within industrial capitalism. The industrial pioneers kept control firmly in their own hands so that the goal of wealth creation was maintained. They looked for the maximum return from their investment and paid the minimum of wages. Since the control of land, machinery and raw material was all in the same hands, all the worker could offer to the 'effort bargain' was his or her labour. When any job has to be taken in order to stay alive, this is no longer exchange but compulsion.

6 Emil Brunner, *Justice and the Social Order* (Lutterworth, 1945) pp 40-46, 50-52, 63-70.

Power and Moral Responsibility

The power with which we have been created to achieve things together carries a responsibility which is not only managerial but also moral. In the second creation story the first people are told not to take the fruit of the tree of the knowledge of good and evil. According to Von Rad this means that they are not to take to themselves the right to decide what is good and what is evil.[7] That remains God's prerogative. It is our responsibility to use our power to do what God says is good for the world.

The history of humankind is a history of the spoiling of the creation pattern through sin. According to Genesis 3 this leads to a breakdown of the God-created relationships between people and God, people and people, and people and nature. By contrast with the order of creation, the fall spells out to us that work is a paradox. It no longer provides satisfaction in the privilege and dignity of 'creative management.' Rather, it is necessary simply to stay alive at all, sweating to work the ground which God has cursed (Genesis 3.17-19). All human work lies somewhere on the spectrum between these two extremes.

Power has been wrongly used in several ways:

1. To Remove from Workers Responsibility for the Work Task.

It is here that serious questions need to be asked by Christians about the patterns of work relationships developed in industrial-capitalist society. We need not suppose that the world must be divided up into postage stamp sized plots for each individual to work. However, we must note, as fundamentally Christian, the right of all to a stake in sharing responsibility for the work enterprise. As Emil Brunner put it:

> 'Man cannot really "subdue the earth" unless some fragment of it belongs to him...The man who treads on strange ground, touches strange property at every movement he makes is not a free man.'[8]

The car assembly line was designed to get the maximum output for the minimum of time. It allowed no initiative, no thinking, no creative opportunity on the part of the worker. So it dehumanized people who spent hours of their time working on it. Eventually the car manufacturers came to realize that the morale of their work force was so low that they had to think of better ways of tackling the task. They started to organize work in teams in which people could vary their jobs and exercise some initiative. However, we still have many jobs that do not allow people to act with much responsibility.

There are still patterns of industrial capitalism in which the majority of the work force lack opportunity to share responsibility for planning the task and assessing the results with satisfaction. It is a mark of fallen society when people, in order to obtain a livelihood, are obliged to 'sell' their labour on the terms of those who are 'owners' of God's land and resources, and who control the production

7 G Von Rad, *Genesis* (London: SCM, 3rd Edition, 1972) p 89.
8 Emil Brunner, *op cit*, p 58.

process primarily to fit their own economic ends. Too easily we accept the assumption of Western society that those who have economic power to do so are morally entitled to buy control of resources from the rest of the people (see Amos 5.8). The patterns of capitalism are inherently divisive of the God-created solidarity of humankind. This is the weakness of capitalism. The creation of wealth is frequently not directed to serve the well-being of all.

Other alternatives, however, have not proved more satisfactory, although some positive results have been achieved by cooperatives, such as at Mondragon in Northern Spain.[9] Whatever the division of ownership or control, our creation theology will cause us to insist that all people involved in a work venture should have the sense that they have a real stake in it and that their well-being is an integral part of its goal.

2. To Deny the Opportunity to Work as a Means of Income.

The normal human way to check the misuse of power is to bring *power against power*. Not surprisingly, in the history of industrial capitalism the workers organized themselves in trade unions to give themselves power to pursue a different and neglected aim, namely their own well-being. This gave to industry a fundamentally conflictive structure in which each side endeavoured to exercise power over the other in pursuit of its aim. The tendency then is for gradual escalation of these conflictive structures. However, because people needed jobs in Britain during the Thatcher years, the power of the trade unions declined.

It needs to be emphasized that both aims—creation of wealth and human well-being—are firmly rooted in the pattern of God's creation. Wherever possible the way forward should be by agreement as to common aims. Otherwise the misuse of power remains a strong possibility. Trade unions can play a very positive role, and if we are without them we shall see a return to harsh and exploitative structures of employment.

3. To Develop Things Which Benefit Some at the Expense of Others.

The work of the worldwide relief agencies has provided many examples of how meeting financial obligations to Western banks, has led to policies in underdeveloped countries which do not benefit their own populations. The manufacture and sale of arms to such countries is another example of a policy which is questionable when the interests and well-being of all are considered.

4. To Pursue Activities Which Jeopardize the Earth's Resources

Such is the created corporateness of humanity that the work process should always have in mind the well-being of humanity the world over and for future generations. The destruction of the Brazilian rain forests is the 'cause celebre' here.

9 The facts about Mondragon are available in the BBC TV Horizon documentary, *The Mondragon Experiment*.

Appeal to Righteousness

The great drawback of 'power against power' is that the issues of righteousness are quickly lost sight of in the struggle for power. Both sides concentrate on increasing their advantage in pursuit of their aims. Reunion is difficult since aims which belong together are set over against each other.

The alternative is to *appeal to righteousness*. This is the way the powerless person challenges the powerful, as Nathan did David, with an appeal to the king's conscience about taking Uriah's wife, Bathsheba (2 Sam 12). It belongs to our human nature that we have to give ourselves moral legitimation for what we do. Therefore the powerful are always vulnerable to the appeal to do with their power what is self-evidently right. Here is a way forward for Christians, for prophetic people, for people of good will when they do not feel they have power to bring about changes. They can appeal to the powerful to do right. The advantage of this way is that it keeps attention on what is right, rather than on who has the greatest power.

Sometimes with the aid of public opinion, through the media, this avenue can be used to check the powerful in the fields of big business, the large service industries and industry as a whole.

As Christians responding to God's vision we shall never be content with the patterns of the fall. We seek an end of sin. We shall, therefore, press for work patterns to be as near as possible to the pattern of creation, to be those patterns which serve human well-being and bring glory to God.

Questions

1. In my occupation how much participation is allowed in the decisions which affect the aims, the objectives and the work patterns? Are there ways in which this participation could helpfully be encouraged?

2. If there are changes that are needed in the structures of my occupation, in what ways can those with power be encouraged to order things differently?

5

The Purpose of Work III: A Community of Good Relationships

It is not only in the creation accounts that we find clear indications of what God is making human beings to be. The vision of the kingdom of God, running through the Scriptures, also provides insights which are applicable to the circumstances of human work.

The kingdom of God is the dynamic coming of God to put things right. It is a powerful spiritual reality, (that is, Holy Spirit driven), which shows itself in its effect, transforming every aspect of life. It is 'not talk but power' (1 Cor 4.20). It is not confined to Christians. When the Spirit of God moves, and people are caught up in his movement, everything starts to come right. While personal and saving entry into the kingdom needs repentance and new birth, the power and direction of the kingdom are seen in the world when healing, justice and reconciliation are being established. Jesus announced the arrival of the kingdom, but he also taught us to pray for the kingdom. It is both here now and not yet.

Key words about the kingdom are righteousness and peace. It is also eternal and universal, (Isaiah 9.6, 7; Romans 14.17). Righteousness and justice are basically the same in Scripture; they are what God is, and requires people to be—what is right. The word for peace, 'shalom' in Hebrew, is a very rich word meaning 'total harmony.' So the kingdom is a vision of perfection, a kingdom of right relationships—with God, with other people and with nature. This does not make it pure idealism; its presence is here in the world and every step in its direction is important. It is, after all, what Christians are to seek first in their lives (Matt 6.33).

In the workplace, the direction of God's purposes means relationships which are right and based on respect, equal dignity and mutual cooperation. There will be unity and harmony. The humanist Abraham Maslow outlined what he understood as a basic hierarchy of human needs.[10] While these have no firm scientific base they are consistent with the direction of God's purposes for human beings as given in creation and the vision of the kingdom of God. Starting with the most basic they are:

- Physiological needs, such as livelihood
- Safety needs, such as a steady income, good safety procedures;
- Belonging needs, the need to 'belong.'; the sense of being together, in unity. In the past this need was often met more by the trade union than by the firm. Sadly, the present 'hire and fire' patterns are destroying values of loyalty and belonging in business and industry today.
- Self-esteem needs; self-esteem through exercising responsibility and initiative,

10 A H Maslow, *Motivation and Personality* (Harper and Row, 2nd edition, 1970) p 35.

and self-esteem through the recognition of others in reward and praise.
- Self-fulfilment needs; the fulfilment or actualization of my potential, for example, in creativity.

It is not difficult to see these needs as closely related to what has already been said about right patterns in the work place in the light of God's direction as seen in creation and in the vision of the kingdom of God.

Work and Worship

Maslow's most obvious omission is the need for worship. While the creation account does not speak directly of worship, the centrality of worship in God's purposes for human beings comes out clearly in the history of the people of God and the vision of the final kingdom where we see heaven in constant praise (Rev 7.9, 10). It is important, then, to consider how human work is expressed in worship. The failure to give a satisfactory answer to this has led to the worlds of industry and business becoming a spiritual wilderness.

As a person fulfils the stewardship given to them in creation so the worth of God is shown. This worship (or 'worthship') is completed as the person offers to God the result of their work, that which by God's energy they have developed or managed. This requires that a person sees the product of their work, and is able to enjoy it as the outworking of their creativity and to offer it to God. Current patterns of work, however, often serve to destroy this sense of worship.

There is another reason for the poverty of spiritual awareness in the field of work. We have not realized that God is present in all human endeavour; we have failed to grasp his immanence, always being far stronger on his transcendence.

When Israel arrived in Canaan it took centuries for the people to grasp that Yahweh, the God who had delivered them from Egypt, was also the Lord of nature. The Baals of surrounding nations, with their accompanying fertility rites, continued to appeal to Israel until the truth of God as the Lord of nature was grasped. Nowadays, judging by the popularity of harvest festival, we do not find it hard to think of God as Lord of nature. Presumably this is because of the givenness of nature. But we have not yet been able to grasp that God is Lord in the rolling of steel or any other industrial achievement. The industrial product is so obviously the product of human endeavour that the hand of God can only be seen in it as his presence and energy are perceived in all human activity and the energy of the material creation is perceived as in some sense God's energy. We live and move and have our being in him (Acts 17.28). Our creativity is the expression of his creative being through the energy and command he has given us. My work is therefore God's work in the fullest sense. If we are going to reverse the spiritual dryness of our industrial and business worlds we shall need to learn how to celebrate these truths and express them in symbolic acts of worship, preferably at the place of work. In no other way will the essential unity between worship and work be grasped in the consciousness of today's believers.

Worship in work, then, we may understand as:
- Offering my work to God;

- Celebrating a share in God's creative work;
- Seeing God in everything, (his immanence);
- Seeing what God is achieving through my occupation.

Summary

Our theology enables us to say with confidence what God is making human beings to be through work.

In work human beings are to realize their creativity, exercising in unity with others their responsibility as under-managers of God's world. They are to work for the well-being and satisfaction of all, taking delight both in the world God has given, and in the products of their own development of it. Their responsibility is to be drawn out by a close association between their work and their livelihood. They are to worship God offering the product of their work and recognizing the presence of God in all that they do.

Although these truths belong to the revelation of Christian theology, they are self-evident truths about what is right for people, with the exception of the truth about worship. They are made known in natural as well as in revealed theology, and discerned by those who are sensitive to basic human rights. As Christians in the work environment we may therefore urge these directions upon our fellow citizens without invoking the name of God as justification for our assertions. It is vital that we win respect for a positive contribution to the issues concerning which our society searches for a solution. Our understanding of what God is making human beings to be we have the basis for just such a positive contribution.

We shall, however, remain realists. The patterns of the fall will persist with us until the Last Day. The fall has many manifestations in the pattern of work in our society and all of them bring their own inherent pattern of judgment. Those who group workers together for efficient production but without security find that, in their solidarity, the workers can obstruct production more effectively. Those who restrict the responsibility of the workers find that the low trust reaps its reward at the negotiating table. Those who urged consumer spending and the attraction of material goods wonder why, when it no longer suits them economically to employ so many, the frustrated unemployed, with no purchasing power, resort to vandalism. Those who have set their heart on a greater share of the cake for their own members find that there is no longer any cake at all.

Another possible reason for the harvest of vandalism in our society is that the kind of work the parents of the vandals were required to do failed to draw out the potential for creative and responsible development of God's world. Instead it bred a dullness of spirit and a rampant desire for material goods and pleasures. In homes where this spirit rules the day many of our young people were raised.

God is not mocked; unrighteousness reaps its own harvest. For that reason the people of God must seek constantly the best patterns of work in our society. Every effort must be made to return to a Godward, creational and community-based understanding of work from one that is privatized and seeks primarily to enhance personal wealth and social standing.

My Commitment to God in my Daily Occupation: Suggested Outline

I wish to seek the kingship of God in my daily occupation. This means:

1. I recognize that God has placed me in my situation and my part in his purpose there is...
2. The vision I have for the coming of the kingdom in the place of my daily occupation is that there will be...
3. In order to see my situation positively I need to have the following attitudes towards other people...
4. In order to look for the kingdom of God in my work situation I offer the following constructive criticism of the aims and patterns of work there...
5. To offer my daily work in worship and celebrate God's presence in it I will...
6. I will pray regularly for the kingdom of God to grow in the place of my daily occupation. (You may like to say how often.)

You may like to sign your commitment.

6

Addressing These Issues in the Parish

Firm initiatives must be taken in parishes if we wish to see develop a spiritual understanding of all daily occupations.

Church Services

The subject is of such importance that it needs to be given a specific focus in the main Sunday service on a reasonably regular basis. More than a mention in the intercessions is necessary; there needs to be an opportunity for thinking through the aim of those occupations and the quality of the work patterns for human fulfilment. A 'work service,' say about every six months, might include:

- an interview with a church member about their personal work situation. Questions such as those in the centre pages of this booklet can then be raised.
- a sermon showing how that particular occupation serves the purposes of God for the well-being of all and where questions need to be raised about whether its work patterns fall short of God's direction. It is wise for the preacher to meet beforehand with representatives of this occupation in order to consider possible material for the sermon.
- a time of intercession to include prayer for all whose occupation is in a particular sphere—education, law, service industries or professions, caring professions, homemakers, retired and so on. Those for whom prayer was focused could be asked to stand or raise a hand so that the rest of the congregation knew for whom they were praying.

- suitably chosen hymns, readings, collect and a Thanksgiving Preface, perhps written specially.

As a variant on this, we held a series in Holy Trinity, Coventry in 1984, entitled 'My Work As God's Work.' Members of the congregation were divided according to the areas of their occupations. Each group was then asked to meet to plan a service, choosing hymns and intercessions and other features such as:

- an exhibition showing the occupations of the members of the group.
- a symbolic offering of this work to God, in the offertory procession.
- in association with the clergy, the sermon and associated readings.

In some cases lay people gave the sermon. Issues relating to the work situations were considered by the group.

The series was a great success and gave rise to something of a carnival atmosphere from week to week. On the first week, a member of the industry group obtained a Metro Moritz to stand at the back of the church as part of the exhibition. When those associated with law did their service one of the participants in the offertory procession wore a judge's wig. The point about God's concern for our daily occupations was certainly made and participants valued the opportunity to meet in groups of those facing similar issues.

Midweek Courses

It is hoped that this booklet will provide a resource for group work in parishes, along the lines suggested on page 14. There is plenty of scope for role play, case studies and the like to help people to feel the strength of the difficulties.

James Jones arranged a midweek series of meetings for Emmanuel, South Croydon in which those with different occupations in the congregation let the congregation in on the pressures and tensions experienced in their work and how they as Christians coped. Each group met to prepare carefully beforehand.

Alternatively, a midweek series can cover biblical themes giving direction to God's purpose for daily occupations and some of the more ethically difficult decisions that have to be made. Group work at these larger meetings can divide people for discussion according to the nature of their occupation. Clear questions in such groups will be necessary to avoid participants simply having a mutual grumbling session. But there should also be occasions for cross-fertilization between occupations. Questions like those in the centre pages can be used by way of preparation. We have added to it questions such as:

> 'Write down any Bible passages which come to mind as being relevant to your particular occupation.'

It is difficult to overstate the relief and appreciation felt by many people when they are given the opportunity to consider these issues. People in the hot seat, in business or elsewhere, are always glad when their dilemmas are understood and not misrepresented.

Pastoral Visits

It is very much appreciated when the pastor takes the trouble to visit members of the congregation in their work places. James Jones shadows people through a typical day. Most people are only too pleased to arrange for the pastor to be shown round the establishment or have him or her drop in on the office. This allows time to listen to what people have to say about their situation, and informs discussion of the purposes of God in that occupation. Such visits also provide excellent illustrative material for sermons. Preaching is more likely to hit the mark if it is addressing hopes, fears and anger that people are known to have.

An Area Course

More recently, in Willesden, we held an all day Lay Congress with about three delegates from each of 86 parishes. The theme was 'My Work as God's Work?' All delegates were asked to fill in the questionnaire before coming. Group leaders were trained beforehand. There were five items in the day:

(i) Opening address, along the lines of the material in this paper.

(ii) Groups organized by occupations, wherever possible. The material for the groups was the filled-in questionnaires. Group members shared their answers first in pairs so as to make sure all engaged with the issues. Discussion in the whole group then followed.

(iii) A presentation through the eyes of Industrial Mission chaplains on where the pain is in the field of work in London at present. Their experience gives them a great deal of experience on which to draw and parishes are sadly slow to make use of their resources.

(iv) Groups organized randomly to discuss the issues raised by the presentation and ask what could be done in the local churches to raise these issues.

(v) A concluding eucharist in which the intercessions were related to issues as indicated by the groups, (each group was asked to state one key issue in the present scene).

The congress was very warmly received and opened up understanding which many had not encountered before. It had extra poignancy as the closure of 31 coal mines had just been announced. We took the opportunity to pass a resolution calling for a reconsideration and sent it to appropriate MPs and public figures.

Following the congress a five week parish course was produced for use in home groups. It includes taped excerpts of both the address and presentation at the congress and a further address on the vision of the kingdom of God as applied to my place of work. The group spends time planning a service to be held some weeks after the course ends, with the cooperation of the incumbent. This gives the group a project to work on together.

Question

Since the church is a sign to the world of the kingdom of God how do we bring to the attention of the Christian community issues at work, such as wrong values and the misdirection of power? How does all this get a hearing in the local church?